This book belongs to

____

My mom said she doesn't TOOT
but I don't know if that's true.
I want to try and catch her,
I'll put it on my things to do.

To-Do
MAKE BED
FIND ROCKS
BUILD A FORT
DESTROY ROOM
CATCH MOM FARTING

I'd hide while she makes breakfast
or sneak in while she folds clothes.
I could feed her some broccoli.
I'll just ask dad, he probably knows.

I've been hiding all day
and haven't heard a peep.
So I went to my mom and asked
"mom do you toot? It's a secret I'll keep"
She said
NO WAY!!!
I don't do that!
Mom was walking around
then on the chair she sat.

Came from her chair.
She looked at me and I looked at her
and we both started to stare.

I said "Uh, mom...WHAT WAS THAT?"
She said "What are you talking about?
It must've been THAT DARN CAT!"

Luckily, dad walked in and
that's when I said,
"Dad do you think mom FARTS?"
He stood there scratching his head.

BLEEP
WAAARRP
Poot
"Hmmm, well...
that's a great question son.
I've heard some pretty weird noises
coming from your moms bum."

She always says
it was probably the CAT
or that it was a squeak
from slipping on the MAT.

She has never said
"Yes, I do actually FART!"
She will just say it was probably
the wheel on the grocery cart.

Later that day
I was having a picnic with mom,
when all of a sudden
it sounded like an ATOMIC BOMB.

BRRRAAAPP!
It came from her butt.
I heard it with my own ears.
It was so stinky
my eyes were filling up with tears.

She can't hide it or say it was from the cat. WAIT... I didn't think girls could do SOMETHING LIKE THAT.

There was no denying it
she had been caught.
Her face was bright red,
then said she actually farted A LOT.

"I fart when I make breakfast
and while I fold the clothes
Even when I eat broccoli.
Just ask your dad, he definitely knows."

She said "unlike your dad
mine are SBDs."
So I took one tiny smell
and fell down to my knees.

"But you are a girl!
YOU CAN'T JUST RIP ONE!
Dad and I are guys,
we do it just for FUN!"
CLAP
BLORT
THURBT
BLAP
GWUMP

"I'm going to act like you didn't CUT THE CHEESE. Can we act like yours aren't silent but deadly.. pretty please?"

She's a mom.
She's not a dad.
She can't lift and toot!
That's not good.. THIS IS BAD.
SNIFF SNIFF
SNIFF SNIFF
POOT
Dad can do it
anywhere he goes.
He does it here and there.
It slightly burns my nose.

AAUUGH
TOOT
But if she does it
a couple times a week
I will start to PANIC,
I'm afraid I WILL START TO STINK!

If i'm around her too much
the stink will get to my clothes!
No one will want to be around me.
They will spray me with a HOSE!

I know it isn't fair
that she has to hold it in.
It's not something I'm used to.
GIRLS FARTING SHOULD BE A SIN.

Mommies are so sweet
and they are so kind.
THE THOUGHT OF THIS
IS BLOWING MY MIND.

PLAP
But here she is,
letting them RIP.
I need to get it together,
I need to get a GRIP.
BIP
BLAT
POOT
SNOOT

I'm trying to accept that her butt whispers. I just THANK GOD I don't have any sisters.

BARK

What happens when friends come to play? If they hear her butt BARK, what will they say?

DO THEIR MOMS DO IT TOO?
DO THEIR DADS CARE?
I have so many questions
I need to clear the air.

I asked Weston and
he said he hasn't heard it yet,
and when I asked Jackson
HE WAS SO UPSET.

He couldn't even talk about it.
He didn't know what to say.
I told him what I knew
And he started to turn grey.

He thought what I thought
and he said what I said.
He feels lied to, they should
have told us. **WE FEEL MISLED.**

**WHAT DO WE DO NOW?
DO WE JUST MOVE ON?**
Maybe we accept the
STINKY FARTS and carry-on.

I know!
I'll forget what I smelled
and that my eyes are now burned.
Although, my mom toots A LOT
I'm still slightly concerned.

THE
END